Raintree is an imprint of Capstone Global Library Limited, a company incorporated in England and Wales having its registered office at 7 Pilgrim Street, London, EC4V 6LB – Registered company number: 6695582

www.raintree.co.uk
myorders@raintree.co.uk

Edited by Penny West
Designed by Steve Mead
Original illustrations © Capstone Global Library Ltd 2015
Picture research by Tracy Cummins
Production by Victoria Fitzgerald
Originated by Capstone Global Library Ltd
Printed and bound in China by Leo Paper Group

ISBN 978 1 406 28750 9
18 17 16 15 14
10 9 8 7 6 5 4 3 2 1

British Library Cataloguing in Publication Data
A full catalogue record for this book is available from the British Library.

Spilsbury, Louise and Richard
Atlantic Ocean. – (Oceans of the World)

Acknowledgements
We would like to thank the following for permission to reproduce photographs: Alamy: Jack Sullivan, 22; Getty Images: Michael Patrick O'Neill, 27 Top, Peter Johansky, 23, Werner Van Steen, 10; Newscom: ICHARD B. LEVINE, 20; Shutterstock: Anton Ivanov, 12, Binu Mathew, 17, Dave Head, 13, Dennis Tokarzewski, 4, Dennis van de Water, 14, Ethan Daniels, Cover Bottom, Giancana, 21, leonello calvetti, Cover Middle, Maisna, 7 Top, meunierd, 26 Left, Richard Bowden, 24, Richard Goldberg, 19, Targn Pleiades, 25, tr3gin, 15, Ugo Montaldo, 18, Wesley Cowpar, Cover Top, Zmiter, Design Element.

We would like to thank Michael Bright for his invaluable help in the preparation of this book.

Contents

Some words are shown in bold, **like this**. You can find out what they mean by looking in the glossary.

About the Atlantic Ocean

The Atlantic is the second biggest ocean in the world. An ocean is a huge area of water. Oceans are different from rivers and lakes because they contain salty water, not fresh water. We cannot drink salty water!

The Atlantic Ocean covers about one-fifth of the Earth's surface.

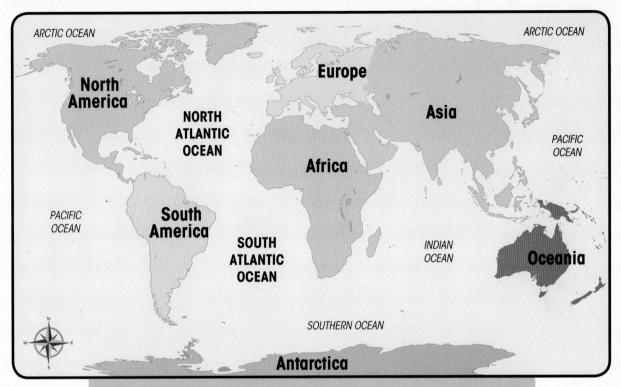

ARCTIC OCEAN

ARCTIC OCEAN

North America

NORTH ATLANTIC OCEAN

Europe

Asia

PACIFIC OCEAN

Africa

PACIFIC OCEAN

South America

SOUTH ATLANTIC OCEAN

INDIAN OCEAN

Oceania

SOUTHERN OCEAN

Antarctica

The Atlantic Ocean is so big that people often divide it into the North Atlantic and South Atlantic.

There are five oceans in the world. The five oceans are joined and water moves between them.
The oceans are mostly divided up by the seven **continents**. To the west of the Atlantic Ocean lie the continents of North America and South America. To the east lie the continents of Europe and Africa.

The Atlantic Ocean is made up of **seas**.
A sea is a smaller area of an ocean
found near the land. Seas are also partly
surrounded by land. The Caribbean Sea,
Baltic Sea and North Sea are all seas in
the Atlantic Ocean.

This map shows some of
the seas of the Atlantic
Ocean found around the
coasts of Europe.

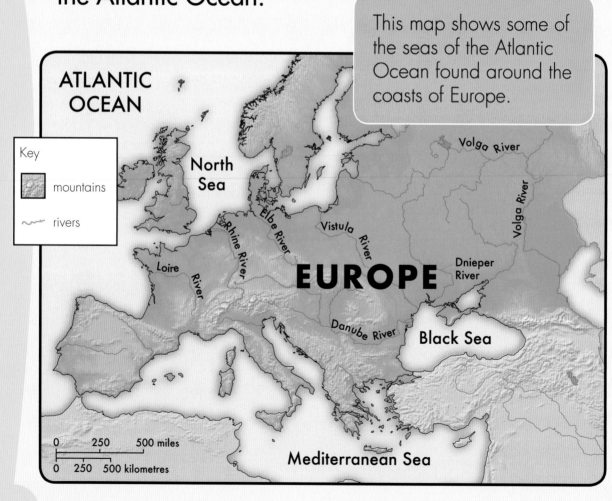

Gulf of
Mexico
Mexico
Cuba

The Gulf of Mexico is on the coast of Mexico, the USA and Cuba.

There are **gulfs** in the Atlantic Ocean, too. A gulf is an area of ocean that is almost completely surrounded by land. The Gulf of Mexico is the largest gulf in the world.

Geography

The Atlantic Ocean is very deep. At the bottom of the Atlantic there are vast, flat areas of ground covered in sand, mud and rock. There are also deep **valleys** or cracks in the ground called trenches.

Atlantic Ocean fact file	
Total area of water:	106,400,000 square kilometres (41,100,000 square miles)
Average depth:	3,300 metres (10,925 feet)
Maximum depth:	8,380 metres (27,493 feet), Milwaukee Deep in the Puerto Rico Trench
Widest point:	6,400 kilometres (4,000 miles), between Cape Horn and the Cape of Good Hope

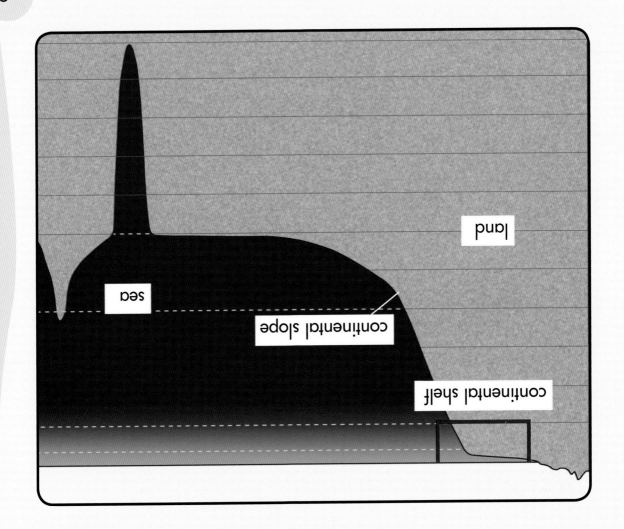

The Atlantic Ocean is shallower at the edge of the **continents**. This is the **continental shelf**. The edge of the shelf slopes down into the deep **sea**. This is the **continental slope**.

The biggest feature on the Atlantic Ocean floor is the S-shaped **mountain range** called the Mid-Atlantic Ridge. It is about 16,000 kilometres (10,000 miles) long and runs almost the entire length of the ocean. It is part of a massive mountain range, the mid-ocean ridge system, which runs around the world.

This diver is exploring the Silfra Crack in Iceland.

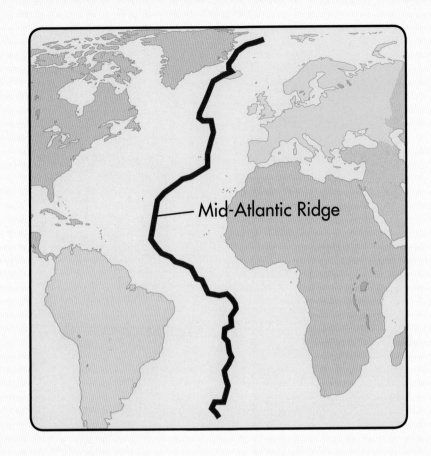

Mid-Atlantic Ridge

The ocean floor around the Mid-Atlantic Ridge is growing. That's because hot, liquid rock from underground comes out close to the ridge and flows to either side. When this rock cools and hardens, it forms new ocean floor. This is making the Atlantic Ocean 2.5 centimetres (an inch) wider each year!

Weather

The temperature of the Atlantic is different in different places. The middle of the Atlantic is near the **Equator**. The sun's rays are more focused here, so the surface of the ocean is mostly warm.

These are the warm, sunny waters of the Caribbean Sea, near the Equator.

The Atlantic coast in winter is stormy and cold.

In the north and south, the Atlantic is cooler and gets even colder closer to the **Poles**. In the winter, the cold **seas** of the north Atlantic get whipped up by strong winds. These can bring high waves crashing onto the coast in places like the UK and USA.

Islands

There are many islands in the Atlantic Ocean. An island is an area of land that is surrounded by water. The largest island in the Atlantic Ocean is Greenland. The Azores are islands formed from the tops of mountains in the Mid-Atlantic Ridge that poke above the water.

Whales swim in the deep waters off the Azores islands.

The Isle of Man is an island in the Irish Sea, which is part of the Atlantic Ocean. It is one of the British Isles.

The British Isles are a group of islands off the north-western coast of the **continent** of Europe. The British Isles includes the islands of Great Britain, Ireland and more than 5,000 small islands!

There are around 7,000 islands in and around the Caribbean Sea. Some of these islands are so small that no one lives on them. The Bahamas, Jamaica and other islands are home to millions of people. The biggest island in the region is Cuba.

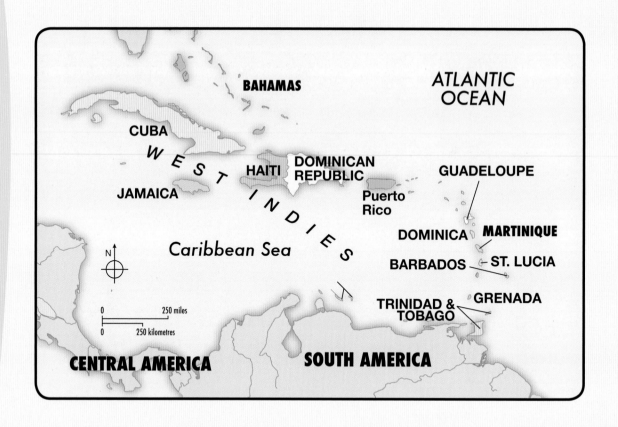

Punta Cana in the Dominican Republic has beautiful sandy beaches to visit.

The Caribbean islands lie near the **Equator** so the ocean here is very warm. Lots of people come to these islands for holidays. They like to lie on the sandy beaches and swim in the ocean.

Resources

One of the most valuable resources in the Atlantic Ocean is fish. People catch fish such as cod, haddock, herring and mackerel here. Atlantic cod and Atlantic bluefin tuna are in danger of dying out because people have caught so many of them.

Tuna swim in vast shoals in the Atlantic.

This oil rig has a huge drill to reach oil from under the ocean floor in the Gulf of Mexico.

We also get oil and natural gas from under the Atlantic Ocean. People drill down into the **continental shelves** to collect a lot of the fuel we use for cars, cooking and heating. In the USA, there are **oil rigs** in the Gulf of Mexico.

Ports

A **port** is a place at the edge of an ocean where ships stop. New York has a big, busy port. The water here is very deep, so giant cargo ships can load and unload containers of goods safely.

The port of New York is on the east coast of North America.

Lisbon lies on the Atlantic coast of southwest Europe.

The port of Lisbon in Portugal is a very busy port on the Atlantic coast of Europe. Every year around 400,000 passengers get off cruise ships to visit the city of Lisbon.

People

More than half of the people in the world live along coasts. In fact, many towns develop around shipping **ports**. In the Gambia some people live in small villages along the Atlantic coast. They build wooden boats to catch fish from the ocean.

Tanji is a large fishing village in the Gambia and many people come here to buy fish.

People live in these floating homes because they like to have a view of the ocean.

Some people have homes on the Atlantic Ocean. Some live in boats that have rooms inside. Others live in floating homes. In New Jersey, USA, some homes float on the water and are tied to the land. Others are built on sturdy posts set deep into the ground under the water.

Animals

There are lots of different animals in the Atlantic Ocean. Atlantic grey seals have a thick layer of fat called **blubber**. This stops them getting too cold in the ocean. They hold their breath and dive down deep to catch fish to eat.

Grey seals leave the ocean and come ashore to rest and have pups.

These Atlantic puffins have caught fish for their young to eat.

There are also sharks, whales, jellyfish and many seabirds. Atlantic puffins are small seabirds that live most of their lives on the Atlantic Ocean. They use their wings to fly and also to swim down deep.

Famous places

The Panama Canal was built through the narrow strip of land called Panama that joins North and South America. The canal allows ships to travel quickly between the Atlantic and Pacific Oceans without going all the way around South America.

ATLANTIC OCEAN

Gulf of Mexico

Panama Canal

South America

PACIFIC OCEAN

The Panama Canal allows cargo ships to cut thousands of miles off their journeys.

The Sargasso Sea is named after the huge amounts of sargassum seaweed that float on its surface.

The Sargasso Sea is the only **sea** in the world that is not near land. This huge sea is surrounded by **currents** that flow clockwise around it and keep the sea in one place.

Sargasso Sea

Gulf of Mexico

Fun facts

- The Sargasso Sea is 1,100 kilometres (700 miles) wide and 3,200 kilometres (2,000 miles) long.

- Ships travelling between the east and west coasts of America shorten their trip by about 15,000 kilometres (9,320 miles, 8,000 nautical miles) by using the Panama Canal!

- The Atlantic Ocean is about half the size of the Pacific Ocean.

- The *Titanic* was the biggest ship in the world when it was built and people said it would never sink. But on its first trip from the UK to America in 1912 it hit an iceberg in the Atlantic Ocean and sank.

Quiz

1 What is the biggest feature on the floor of the Atlantic Ocean?

2 Which is the largest **gulf** in the world?

3 Which is the largest island in the Atlantic Ocean?

4 How many islands are there in and around the Caribbean Sea?

Glossary

blubber thick layer of fat under an animal's skin

continent one of seven huge areas of land on Earth

continental shelf (more than one are called **continental shelves**) part of a continent that is underwater

continental slope where land off the coast of a continent slopes under deep ocean

current body of water moving in one direction

Equator imaginary line around the middle of the Earth

gulf part of an ocean that extends into the land

mountain range group or chain of mountains that are close together

oil rig platform with a drill that can drill underground to collect oil

Poles the two points at opposite ends of the Earth, the North Pole and South Pole

port place at the edge of an ocean where ships stop

sea smaller area of an ocean usually found near the land and usually partly surrounded by land

valley long, narrow and deep groove in the land

Find out more

Books

Deep Oceans (Earth's Last Frontiers), Ellen Labrecque (Raintree, 2014)

Ocean (Eyewitness), Miranda MacQuitty (Dorling Kindersley, 2014)

Ocean Food Chains (Food Chains and Webs), Angela Royston (Raintree, 2014)

Ocean Wildlife (Saving Wildlife), Sonya Newland (Franklin Watts, 2011)

What Happens if we Overfish the Oceans? (Unstable Earth), Angela Royston (Wayland, 2013)

Websites

Videos, images and facts about the deep ocean can be found at
www.bbc.co.uk/nature/habitats/Deep_sea

You'll find lots of fun facts at
www.fun-facts.org.uk/earth/ocean.htm

You'll find lots of interesting facts about the world's oceans at
www.savethesea.org/STS%20ocean_facts.htm

Index